)))))))))

Raves for Perception

(It's never too late to learn)
"One thing I learned during my years as CEO is that perception matters. And in these times when public confidence and trust have been shaken, I've learned the hard way that perception matters more than ever."
Jack Welch, former CEO and Chairman, General Electric, Wall Street Journal, 9/16/02

(If you don't at first succeed...)
"It took us a long time to get into the rankings because of the perception that we were a young team that wasn't going to be ready."
Jim Boeheim, Syracuse basketball coach, on CBS after winning the NCAA Championships, 4/7/03

(Understatement of the year)
"Perception, perception, perception . . . this will go down badly."
Dennis Kozlowski Former CEO of Worldcom New Yorker magazine, 2/17/03

(Advice for Martha Stewart)
"The solution to stress management lies in how we perceive the stresses in our lives."
Doc Childre and Howard Martin The HeartMath Solution

(On Nike's failure to dominate golf equipment)
"The company has not been able to persuade golfers, well schooled by Callaway, to look at a Big Bertha without feeling an extra ten yards coming."
Douglas B. Holt, Ass't Professor,
Harvard Business School
New Yorker letter-to-the editor, 7/15/02

(Dedicated to Warren Buffett and Bill Gates)
Money itself isn't lost or made, it's simply transferred from one perception to another."
Oliver Stone, American filmmaker

(Conversations with God)
"I think you will agree that perception is more important than reality."
Mark Haynes, Host of CNBC's Squawk Box,
discussing the SARS virus, 4/28/03

(Tip for re-branding consultants)
"An optimist sees an opportunity in every calamity. A pessimist sees a calamity in every opportunity."
Sir Winston Churchill, British statesman

(Compassion for the makers of the Edsel)
Everyone has beauty, but not everyone sees it."
Confucious, Chinese philosopher

(Diversity inspiration)
"You never really understand a person until you consider things from his point of view...until you climb inside of his skin and walk around in it."
Harper Lee, To Kill a Mockingbird

(Saving American Airlines from bankruptcy)
The popularity of disaster movies...expresses a collective perception of a world threatened by irresistible and unforeseen forces which nevertheless are thwarted at the last moment."
David Mamet, American playwrite

(Dedicated to Bill O'Reilly)
"The intention of psychoanalysis is to strengthen the ego, to make it more independent of the superego, to widen its field of perception..."
Sigmund Freud, Austrian psychiatrist

(Windex award)
"Better keep yourself clean and bright; you're the window through which you must see the world."
George Bernard Shaw, Irish playwrite

THIS BOOK IS
DEDICATEDTO
MAMA OTEY,
CREATOR OF
WICKED WYOMING
CHICKEN MARINADE

Published by BullsEye, LLC

For information about books in the PERCEPTION RULES! series,
and BullsEye Branding training and consulting programs and
merchandise, see pages 119-124.

Visit our website at www.perceptionrules.net

First printing, September, 2003

ISBN 0-9744885-1-8

LCCN 2003096171

Printed in the United States of America

Graphic Design by Lyndsay W Beauchamp
Creative Director: V Harris

Table of Contents:

)⟩)⟩)⟩

Preface

In the spring of 2003, I was at Heathrow Airport waiting to board one of the final flights of the Concorde from London to New York. Sitting next to me was the most amazing character I had ever laid eyes on: a coyote dressed to kill, cocky as could be, and full of charm. I knew that this could only be the infamous Kyle Otey, creator of the biggest and most successful chicken conglomerate in branding history.

He was deep in discussion with the former Chairman of G.E., Jack Welch, about golf in Scotland. They were talking about perception and I was fascinated with Kyle Otey's mastery of its impact on how great brands are made, unmade, and saved.

I introduced myself as a writer who found Kyle Otey's insights about branding and perception to be brilliant. One thing led to another, and shortly after returning to the States, Kyle Otey introduced me to Brandin the Bull, the new symbol of success on Wall Street. I wrote Brandin's life story as the first book in my series of self-help and business books called PERCEPTION RULES!

While the *Story of Brandin the Misunderstood Bull* deals with the role that perception plays in personal success, the *Widsom of Kyle Otey* is based on the Chicken Billionaire's renowned lectures to the Harvard Business School. In no-nonsense, down-to-earth language Kyle Otey reveals how the 7 Rules of Perception control branding from a marketing perspective. His insights break new ground and usher in needed understanding about the very complex and misunderstood subject of branding, the biggest buzz word in business today.

I am indebted to Kyle Otey for asking me to collaborate on writing this book. And I hope that Jack Welch likes it.

V Harris
September, 2003

V HARRIS

Introduction

(One fine, fall day not so long ago, the auditorium at Harvard Business School was packed with eager, budding, MBA brains waiting breathlessly to hear the wisdom of Kyle Otey.

Kyle Otey: A living legend...a starving coyote who rose to head the world's biggest chicken conglomerate. Bigger than Perdue!

The story of this lone innovator's rise to the heights of power and success is a veritable text book case of what you do (and don't do) to become a brand leader. And that is why on this fine, fall day the students of Harvard Business School sit in rapt silence waiting for their hero to enter the hall.

The house lights dim. The curtain rises. And there, standing in a lone spotlight is Kyle Otey himself, hand on hip, lips curled in a now world famous smirk.

The smirk of a billionaire!)

Oh sit down, for cripes sakes! And shut off those damn cell phones! I'm here to give you an earful about this thing called branding.

As we coyote's say, "let's cut to the chase." Branding is one of the most bandied about, and misused words in business today. Ask ten people the question, what is branding? and you'll get 10 different answers – and they're all wrong! Some dummy in Washington even said that they were branding Tom Ridge. Dot coms thought they could create instant brand leaders. Instant? What the hell does that mean? You tell me!

These days, everyone wants to be a brand leader, build brand equity and brand loyalty. But just saying the words has as much credibility as Bernie Ebbers' or Dennis Kozlowski's name on a Harvard diploma! Poor Bernie and Dennis – but, I'll get to them later.

First let me make one thing clear.
When all is said and done:

Branding is the control of perception.

That is the simplest explanation that you're ever going to hear from anyone.

It was a comment about perception that inspired me to do these lectures, in fact. My buddy, Jack Welch and I were returning to the states after playing golf in Scotland, and

I happened to pick up a copy of the *New Yorker* magazine. There was this letter to the editor by an Assistant Professor of Marketing at Harvard Business School named Doug Holt. You know Doug. Well, he wrote that Calloway's dominance over Nike in golf clubs is because Nike "has not been able to persuade golfers, well schooled by Callaway, to look at a Big Bertha without feeling an extra ten yards coming."

"Perception!" I shouted with glee. "Didn't I tell you, Jack, that perception is a monster concept that brings even the biggest gurus down to their knees!" Jack and I had a good chuckle because we both learned the hard way about the power of perception.

But I'm getting ahead of myself. First, I want to tell you about my boyhood out in Wyoming. Coyotes everywhere and not a damn thing to eat. My mother, Mama Otey, god rest her soul, tried her best to feed us, but times they were tough. So, don't moan to me about how tight the job market is for eager entrepreneurs in this post Enron, post dot-com world that we live in!

Anyway, there I was out in the boonies in Wyoming running myself ragged to find a scrawny rabbit to eat! Then I ran into this bull named Brandin, a nice enough guy who'd been put out to pasture at a nearby ranch. Well, this bull was like no bull I'd ever seen. A real wimp with no backbone. Felt no one understood him.

"Talk about bad perception," I told him, "How'd you like to be seen as some sly, sneaky, shifty varmint that you shoot on sight! So let me get this straight: your big problem is being perceived as a big, mean, scary bull? Well get over it. I say, give the people what they want. In corporate America, the big cheeses are forever playing roles, trying to live up to preconceived notions of power and success."

Well, I'm beginning to get through to Brandin – when out of the blue this Eagle flies in and proceeds to joins the conversation. Didn't take me long to realize that the Eagle had a keen eye for how perception works. The Eagle taught Brandin how to use the 7 Rules of Perception to shape up his image and be seen for who he truly is.

Before I knew it, Brandin was the new symbol of success on Wall Street and the rest is history. People traveled to the ranch in Wyoming to have their picture taken with their new hero, Brandin the Bull. Brandin's story became the best-seller, *PERCEPTION RULES! Personal Success* by V Harris – who also helped me write this book, god bless her.

One day, seeing all the tourists lining up to have their pictures taken with Brandin, I got this idea: why not turn my love of chicken into a product that the tourists would take home. And that's how Wicked Wyoming Chicken Marinade was born based on Mama Otey's secret recipe.

The tourists snapped up the stuff quicker than a starving coyote can say Kentucky Fried Chicken! And before I knew it, Mama, my sisters and brothers, and my 12 kids were bottling the marinade night and day.

But truth be told, we were winging it. **I knew that to become a brand leader, I had to control perception from day one.** So I asked the Eagle to be my marketing consultant. I figured that if the Eagle's 7 Rules of Perception could help Brandin the Bull succeed, they could do the same for the Kyle Otey brand. The BullsEye Branding Method that the Eagle taught me is the reason why I am standing here today as the Chicken Billionaire.

So listen carefully.

Learn the
7 Rules of Perception,
and the BullsEye
Branding Method
like I did.

PART ONE:
THE BASICS

))))))

Chapter One
Perception is Reality

You know the cliché: Perception is Reality. It's been
around as long as coyotes have been chasing chickens.
But what does it mean? Just how does perception work?
And how does it impact brand leadership? Instead of
boring you with a long explanation from the dictionary,
let me give you my own condensed version:

**Perception is based NOT on what you say,
or thought you said...it's what someone else
hears, what they think you meant, and what
they want to believe.**

In Philip Kotler's classic textbook, *Marketing
Management*, perception is defined as: "the process by
which an individual selects, organizes, and interprets
information inputs to create a meaningful picture of
the world."

This involves personal experience that's hard to eradicate.
Some trigger mechanism may kick in a perception based on
something that happened long ago. George Bush Sr. told me
that he still remembers the first time he smelled broccoli!
While it is true that our perceptions can indeed change
over time, once a perception is formed it is difficult to

change. That is why marketers place such importance on brand loyalty. We willingly pay more for, and remain fans of, brands that we know and trust.

Perception determines the branding strength of every business, institution, and organization, large or small.

Issues controlled by perception include:

Brand leadership	Productivity
Marketing and sales	Office politics
Customer service	Employee relations
Risk and change	Public relations
Diversity	Investor relations

Take the vital area of sales. Sales people often complain that if customers only understood how good their product or service is – that if "they only knew the real truth" – sales would pour in.

But, here's the real truth:

How you perceive your business or product is your reality.

How any other person perceives your business or product is their reality.

This is why effective sales people always identify with the customer's point of view while ineffective sales people do not. They moan and groan that a customer misperceives their product, when it is their inability to understand how perception works that is the problem.

The BullsEye Branding Method that the Eagle taught me maintains that perception not only controls the branding strength of every business, institution, and organization,

Perception also controls the success of yours and my Personal Brand.

Call it image, if you like. Personal Branding and Product Branding are remarkably similar. In fact, the 7 Rules of Perception and the BullsEye Branding Method work the same way with both. So, no matter what type of brand you are trying to manage you must first learn what perception is, and how it impacts *your own ability to succeed.*

**How you perceive yourself,
or any other person is your reality.**

How any other person perceives you is their reality, whether fair or not.

Perception impacts every imaginable part of your life – at home, at the office, and in the community.

This includes:
    Communicating effectively
    Building self-respect and self-confidence
    Getting a job, then not losing it
    Buying and selling a house or a car
    Finding a date or a mate
    Controlling weight
    Managing stress
    Coping with death and divorce
    Dealing with disabilities
    Navigating change and aging

You know the expression, "beauty is in the eye of the beholder." At first glance, I may look at a woman and see her as overweight and over made-up, but if her husband thinks she's sexy, SHE IS SEXY!

Take a couple shopping for a car. The husband may see the salesman as knowledgeable, savvy and persuasive, while his wife – in the same meeting with the same salesman – may see him as pushy, phony, and sexist. But try to tell the salesman that.

It is very human to complain about how you are perceived.

On your way to work:
"I'm not who you think I am."
"No one understands me."
"You just don't get it (or me)."
"If she (he) only knew how wonderful
 I am he'd (she'd) date me, or marry me."

At work:
"If you only knew how much I do for you,
  you'd give me a raise."
"No one appreciates how much I contribute
  to the bottom line."
"My boss doesn't listen to me."
"You'll miss me when I'm gone!"

Notice that the way a person complains about how they are perceived sounds the same as a sales person complaining about how the company or product is perceived. Uncanny the similarity. Both are fighting the fact that like it or not, another person's perception may be different from your own.

Believe me, I've done my share of complaining about how coyotes are perceived. Truth be told, in Indian legend we coyotes and wolves were the first healers. I can run at almost 40 mph – which is a good thing because before I became the Chicken Billionaire I spent most of my time alone covering thousands of square miles trying to find a square meal.

Seems the only thing I couldn't outrun was my reputation – for what did people think of me? Not as a clever, resourceful survivor who mates for life and rarely goes after livestock, but as some sly, sneaky, shifty varmint that you shoot on sight! Tell me if that's fair! And speaking of bad raps. Look what the movie *Jaws* did to sharks. Created mass hysteria!

Another example is my American Eagle friend back home in Wyoming – the one who taught me the 7 Rules of Perception. Eagles may look strong and powerful, but their skeletons are hollow and filled with air. Their bones actually weigh less than their 7,000 feathers! But we perceive them as such strong and powerful creatures that they are the national symbol of America!

Here are some of the areas of your life where perception has a powerful impact:

The war on terrorism. Why did we go to war with Iraq? How do you know who the enemy is if they're not wearing a uniform? Is profiling people from Middle Eastern countries acceptable? (And profiling, by the way, is a negative form of Personal Branding).

Attitude. Do you see the glass half empty or half full? What do you worry about? What makes you anxious or afraid? How do you deal with stress?

Weight. Everyone has beauty, but not everyone sees it." Gyms are packed with gals trying to look like J. Lo. and guys like Mel Gibson. "Fat people may be happy people," but perception about obesity is fast-changing in the face of studies showing its disastrous impact on the health of millions of Americans.

Health and wellness. Perception has a dramatic impact on a person's ability to battle diseases such as cancer. Did you know that anorexics perceive that they are fat even as they are starving to death. Then there's the placebo effect. Doctors know how easily our minds can trick us. If we think we've been given a pill that will help us, we feel better – even if the pill was a fake.

The stock market. Investors pay a huge premium for biotech stocks with no earnings. Mutual fund managers "window dress" at the very end of a quarter. Worldcom, Tyco, and Enron cooked their books to keep alive the perception that they could sustain double digit growth. Perception and the market are as intertwined as yin and yang.

Perceived value. You'll pay more for a brand name than its generic counterpart. Is a Ralph Lauren t-shirt really worth five times more than a Wal-Mart t-shirt? Most probably not, but if you perceive something is better, you'll pay more. Conversely, a product priced at $19.99 is perceived as a better deal than the same item for $20.

Politics. In office politics, or any kind of politics, perception often counts more than performance. It impacts getting a job, keeping it once you have it, and getting the raise you think you deserve. Politicians are masters of perception. When President Bush traveled to a plant in middle America in the spring of 2003 to promote jobs with small businesses, he stood in front of crates stamped "Made in America," but the rear side of the crates – the side the TV viewers couldn't see – actually said, "Made in Taiwan." Those political spin-masters know that seeing is believing.

Movie stars know that once the public perceives them a certain way, it's difficult to change their image. When we go to see a John Wayne movie, we want to see John Wayne, not Hannibal Lector! Few actors are allowed to stray beyond "type."

Rule 1:
Perception *is* Reality

How a person perceives any brand is his or her reality (whether fair or not).

))))))

Chapter Two
Powerful Influences

One of the first things that my consultant, the Eagle, taught me was that perception doesn't just happen in a vacuum. There are many powerful influences that impact how our perceptions are formed.

Before you have said or done anything, a person may have already formed a perception of you. Call it intuition, a snap judgment, a sixth sense, stereotyping or profiling, but it happens all the time. I'm not saying that its right, but please – let's be honest about this.

Researchers at a college asked students to rank their professor. They did a semester's worth of video tapes of the professor's lectures and then lost a whole bunch of the tapes. When they analyzed what they had left, they were amazed to discover that how the students perceived the professor at the beginning of the semester did not change. Their minds were made up from the start!

Now the researchers were fascinated. They started studying job interviews. Know what they found? The interviewer makes his or her mind up about a prospect *within five seconds* of their walking into the room! And nothing that the prospect says or does in the interview changes the interviewer's initial perception.

The interviewer's knee-jerk reaction may have been based on his or her gut instincts, personal biases, or stereotypes. Again, I'm not saying that this is fair or correct. What I am saying is that, like it or not, this is the way perception at times works. We can't just dislike something and hope that it goes away. Combating profiling means first understanding how it works.

When an opinion, attitude, or judgment of a person, a race, an issue, or an event is repeated over and over again without variation – until every member of a group shares the same mental image – it becomes a stereotype.

Stereotypes are oversimplified opinions.

So is profiling – which sadly goes on all the time all over the world. People hate to admit this because profiling has so many negative connotations, and negative applications. We coyotes are profiled all the time.

In each and every perception that you form, you bring everything that you have learned, the tiniest details of your past, your conscious and subconscious into play.

Here's what influences how our perceptions are formed.

- *The five senses (from the Latin, senses: the faculty of perceiving) – sight, hearing, smell, touch, and taste.*

- *Race nationality ethnic background*

- *Gender*

- *Age*

- *Personality*

- *Language*

- *Type of work*

- *Income*

- *Place of residence*

- *Marital state and number of children*

- *Sexual orientation*

- *Health – physical and psychological*

- *Emotional make-up, attitude, mood, fears, sensitivities, anxieties, worries, and concerns*

- *Height, weight, shape*

- *Personal appearance – clothing, hair, make-up, jewelry, etc.*

- *Body language, posture, mannerisms*

- *Verbal clues such as tone of voice*

- *Religion – or lack of it*

- *Upbringing*

- *Memories – good and bad*

- *Family views, biases and influences*

- *Level of intelligence*

- *Creativity and imagination*

- *Education – where it took place, who did the educating, and for how long*

- *Reputation*

- *Myth, superstition*

- *The media: books, newspapers, magazines radio, television, films*

- *Views of business, religious, political, and community leaders*

- *What friends and those you admire say, think, eat, drink, drive, and wear*

- *Clubs, organizations, unions, and other affiliations*

Perception, in sum, is based on lot's of assumptions – which may be right or wrong and lots of intangibles – which are often difficult to define.

Rule 2
Powerful Influences

**Many factors
influence how
anyone or
anything
is perceived.**

⟫ ⟫ ⟫

Chapter Three
The Rule of Three

Given all of the many influences that impact how we perceive anything it was absolutely amazing – even shocking – for me to learn that:

The way any product, any business, or any person is *perceived* tends to be reduced to three descriptive words. This is the Rule of Three.

While it is true that more than three words may be used to describe a person, a business, or a product, the subsequent words chosen are still various versions of the first three concepts. For instance, sexy may also be described as alluring, attractive, handsome, beautiful, etc. But all are describing a similar attribute – or deficiency.

Oh, I can hear your minds at work disputing what I've just said. "It just can't be that simple," you're thinking. "I'm much more complex than that, or why am I an MBA student at Harvard?" Well, let me give you some examples of just how true the Rule of Three is:

Early Judaism was founded on the three T's: Torah, Temple and Territory.

Christianity uses the Trinity to describe God as Father, Son and Holy Ghost.

Democracy is summed up as Life, Liberty and the Pursuit of Happiness.

Queen Elizabeth I was "a combination of prudence, boldness and genius," according to her biographer, Alan Axelrod in his fascinating work, *Elizabeth I, CEO.*

President Bush has attained the status of the "Bush Brand" in the eyes of GOP polster, Bill McInturff. The Bush Rule of Three is summed up as: "strong leadership, admirable morals, and a family focus."

Of course we all know that – truth be told – we are terribly complex creatures. And so it is a tad discomforting to realize that how our glorious, complex self is perceived is reduced to three simple, descriptive words. The Rule of Three is truly an humbling experience!

Bill Clinton's complex, contradictory self is summed up with three descriptive words or phrases. All the millions of photo ops, headlines, articles, interviews, and speeches are reduced to The Rule of Three. And those three words that define how he is *perceived* by others are the *reality* of his public image – the strength of his Personal Brand.

In sum: if The Rule of Three is good enough for Judaism, Christianity, the Declaration of Independence, Queen Elizabeth I, George Bush, and Bill Clinton, then it's good enough for you and me.

Rule 3
The Rule of Three

How anything or anyone is perceived tends to be reduced to three descriptive words that may be positive or negative.

PART TWO:
PROOF POSITIVE
(AND NEGATIVE)

∂) ∂) ∂)

Chapter Four
The Ultimate Brand In History

Steve Tisch, the head of the Lowe's chain of hotels, thinks that the #1 brand in the world is the United States. And that may be true right now. But, over a longer period of time – say several thousands of years – I think there's no contest for the ultimate brand. And perception played a very powerful role in its development.

Two thousand years ago, a revolutionary new concept was created in a scrubby area of the Middle East that completely altered the course of human history. The creators of the concept had no power, no money, no influence, no press. What they *did* have was the power of a compelling idea that spread word-of-mouth.

They named their concept Christianity after its leader, Jesus, who was known as the Christ.

Lesson: People often times muck up the potential of their brand by coming up with names that have absolutely nothing to do with the product. A good name relates to the product or service provided and not only supports, but enhances the way it is perceived.

The symbol:

The early leaders of Christianity also created the greatest symbol (marketers call it a logo) in history – namely the cross. From the beginning it was worn on people's bodies, sewn into their clothing, and hung from their carts.

The symbol simply and eloquently identified the basic underlying concept of the new religion – that Jesus died on the Cross as the perfect sacrifice for the sins of the world.

Lesson: a great symbol is a visual manifestation of the basic essence of a brand. It is instantly understandable and memorable.

The slogan:

The brand name (Christianity) and the symbol (the Cross), were then magnificently summed up in three descriptive words that everyone could understand:

Father. Son. Holy Ghost.

The leaders of the new religion made these three words absolute at the Council of Nicea in the year 354. Any competing concepts and ideas about Christianity that had been floating about for the previous three plus centuries were eradicated. Done. Caput! Father. Son. Holy Ghost.

The Rule of Three – the Trinity– was repeated over, and over, and over again in every aspect of the new religion's branding program forever after.

Lesson: a great slogan is brief and to the point. It defines what the brand is or does, and is included in everything produced to promote the way the brand should be perceived.

The mission statement:

The leaders of Christianity wanted everyone to understand the concept of The Father, The Son and The Holy Ghost – particularly given the fact that the most powerful leader of the world at that time, the Emperor Constantine, had become a believer and ordered everyone in his Empire to become instant Christians (and you think Bill Gates has a monopoly)!

The mission statement explains clearly and concisely exactly what Christians believe in – and unlike most missions statements today, it was not just tacked up on the wall of a waiting room. The Christian mission statement – the Apostles' Creed – has been repeated over and over and over again at every single service and celebration for 17 centuries! It is the essence of perception becoming reality.

Lesson: Develop an original (not copycat) mission statement that accurately defines your brand, supports your positioning statement, and differentiates it from the competition – so that how you wish to be perceived becomes reality.

Then have every employee repeat it over and over and over again until they know it by heart.

And have every customer understand it, and believe it.

And know that every one of your competitors will try to copy it and hang it on their waiting room wall.

))))))

Chapter Five
The Biggest Branding Bomb in History

Remember the Edsel? A failure so huge that the name of Ford's radical new auto in the 50's became a veritable cliche for failure. But not good enough to be branding bomb #1 in history.

And the "new" Coke? **Another** of the great branding bombs of all time But still not #1.

The winner? A virtual tie between the failed dot-com upstarts, and scandal-ridden corporate America.

From 1995 to 2000, the dot.coms arrived with breathtaking speed promising to revolutionize the way we buy our food, drugs, furniture, pet food, gardening supplies, toys, run our businesses – you name it. The virtues of the virtual storefront and technology upstarts were hyped with wild abandon. Initial public offerings of companies with no revenues whatsoever came to market with instant valuations in the billions.

Business Week did a cover story on e.biz in August, 2001, and it read:

"Dressed to Kill. *At the height of the dot-com craze, countless companies focused on a single goal: get prettied up for sale."*

Clueless investors poured billions into dot-com companies – and much of it was spent on advertising designed to create the perception of instant branding success. If you were lucky enough to get shares in the IPO of etoys you woke up the next morning an investor in a business valued at $7.5 BILLION! Hopefully you sold your etoys stock right away because etoys was one of the first dot.com bankruptcies.

Perceived value had gone amuck!
And it spilled over to established
Fortune 500 companies.

The "irrational exuberance" of the stock market fueled by greed led to a breakdown in ethical standards in the accounting and legal professions, as well as the financial and investment industries. Integrity and honesty took a vacation while executives at Adelphia Consulting, Enron, Worldcom, Tyco, Global Crossing, Xerox, and the like, cooked the books and fudged figures to keep alive the perception of double digit growth.

CNBC ran a documentary in September, 2003 that summed it all up. It's title? *The Big Lie: Inside the Rise and Fall of Worldcom.*

Auditors, bankers, regulators, boards, and governing bodies alike looked the other way. The SEC, the New York Stock Exchange, the American Stock Exchange, and NASDAQ didn't say a peep. People were making so much money that financial reports that now seem absurd were considered, at the time, perfectly normal. If there weren't any earnings, not to worry. Simply do pro forma reporting. It's perception that counts!

At Super Bowl time, dot-coms – whose names we no longer remember – matched the millions that hallowed brand leaders such as Coke and Andheuser-Busch spent on a 30-second commercial, thinking that by doing so they could create the perception of "instant brand leadership." And what about sales, profits, earnings per share? Forget about it! That's "Old Economy" thinking.

Being perceived as "first to market" was the name of the game. Even the normally sane marketing heads of established brand leaders got caught up in the buzz, and spent **billions** of dollars on sidebars on the internet. For only $30 million you could have an innocuous button on CNet for two years! Who could resist such as deal?

Forget that there was no validity about net advertising being effective; about actual sales resulting from all the money thrown into all of those irritating, repetitive side bars and buttons. The perception was that you had to be a player in this brave new world whatever it took.

Goodbye suits, hello black t-shirts. Dress down or get a dressing down by your techies and a lecture from your board about not adapting quickly enough. Talk about the power of perception! At the press conference announcing the merger of AOL and Time Warner, the new boy on the block, Steve Case, wore a suit, while the Chairman of Time Warner, Jerry Levin, sported a t-shirt! Casual Fridays quickly became Casual Everyday. Good thing Ted Turner didn't throw out his suits because when AOL earnings took a dive, it didn't seem cool to be seen on TV wearing a $200 t-shirt. Hickey-Freeman is thrilled! They know all about suits and the perception of substance.

As the *New York Times* reported on December 21, 2000, "Blinded by the potential for vast new markets...companies and investors alike fell into bad habits that Wall Street only encouraged." The good news reported in the article was that "The Return of Traditional Values" has begun...the days of placing false faith in hype is over...the dot-com bubble has burst. But the binge may take years to cure."

That was three years ago as I write this, and we're not out of the woods yet. Corporate America has real perception problems with Main Street investors who remain skeptical about the market.

Lesson: Once you've lost your customer you must surpass expectations to win them back, and this is very difficult to do.

Chapter Six
It All Borders on Insanity!

Just ask Robert DiRomualdo, Chairman of the Borders Group that includes the national chain of Borders Books and Music stores, and Walden book stores. How he kept his sanity during the dot-com mania is anyone's guess. He knew for sure that perception was totally disconnected from reality.

As the leader of an innovative, fast growing company with over $1 BILLION in annual sales and actual PROFITS – from 1995 to 2000, DiRomualdo had to deal with an almost daily dose of ridicule from the media about how Borders "just didn't get it." Amazon was taking the world by storm. Brick and mortar was suddenly perceived as a thing of the past.

DiRomualdo also had to withstand almost daily pressure from disgruntled employees and members of his board as the value of Borders stock plummeted. In the spring of 2001, with a market cap of $5.5 billion, Amazon was worth more than Borders and Barnes and Noble combined – on actual revenues of only $31 million, LOSSES of a quarter BILLION dollars in *one quarter alone*, and absolutely no profits.

More than 1,000 virtual book stores had opened on the web. DiRomualdo remembers one called Books-A-Million, a two buck stock in the spring of 2000, when a simple little announcement that it had updated its website catapulted its stock price to $47 a share!

You can see why Robert DiRomualdo – despite his long and distinguished career in retailing and his degree from Harvard – saw no rational explanation, no logic whatsoever in investors perceptions about net land. Had all of the basic rules of business and bottom line results gone out the window? Were the rules of financial reporting and profits suddenly meaningless?

Were actual brick and mortar stores suddenly obsolete? It all seems so silly now, doesn't it?

Fortunately, DiRomualdo had the last laugh. In the spring of 2001, he inked a deal with Amazon that instantly produced an enviable "bricks and clicks" combo that actually does make business sense.

Robert DiRomualdo's perception shot up overnight.

Chapter Seven
Jell-O is Jell-O.
And Kleenex is Kleenex.

Mama Otey is a fan of both because what she sees is what she gets.

What she perceives Jello and Kleenex to be is exactly what they are in reality. United. The same. And both companies work hard to make sure it stays that way. They remain consistently and persistently comfortable with who they are and value their relationship with their loyal customers – even though there are cheaper alternatives nearby on the shelf.

Jell-O and Kleenex are two of the strongest and longest lasting brands in history. In fact, how consumers perceive both brands is so positive, and so strong that their names are synonymous with their product category. (Which their lawyers don't like because they must protect trademarks which are lost if the name becomes generic).

Despite this, we ask for Jell-O, not gelatin, and we ask for Kleenex, not facial tissue.

This is the ultimate in brand leadership. Total control of perception.

But is Xerox, Xerox?

Do we know what this company does anymore? They used to be one of the strongest brands in history. So much so that if we wanted a copy, we asked for "a Xerox." We said, "Xerox this please." Even though Xerox's lawyers tried to get us to ask for a Xerox copy, not just a Xerox.

But how times have changed! Xerox had a difficult time adapting from copiers to the digital world, and in the process lost control of perception.

As their enviable brand equity suffered massive erosion – and the value of their stock dropped – its top executives only made matters worse. I'll speak about this later in Chapter 18.

The handwriting was on the wall when with great fanfare they created their new, red X symbol featuring digitized bits spinning off into space. The symbol actually revealed their own internal disintegration.

Xerox is a classic case of a brand gone bad.

PART THREE:
SAY GOODBYE
TO BRANDING B.S.

⁍ ⁍ ⁍

Chapter Eight
I just don't get it!

"Branding" is THE biggie in business – the buzz word of our times – bandied about endlessly in marketing departments and ad agencies, board rooms and business schools.

Every business today wants to be a brand leader, build brand loyalty and brand equity, and prevent brand erosion,

But,

ask ten people what the word "branding" means, and you'll get ten different answers.

Branding is, in fact, one of the most misunderstood, misused, and abused words in corporate America today.

Here are some quotes from a book called *Warp Speed Branding* – you've gotta love the title! It was one of many books that created perceptions in the minds of marketers that had no basis in reality.

Here are just a few examples:

Brand managers no longer "narrowly focus" on "product improvements, promotions, packaging and advertising."
Just where do they focus then? On T-shirt sales?

"The world of mass manufacturing, mass distribution, and mass merchandising is over." Wal-Mart, Target, and Nordstrom please take note!

"The brand can no longer be controlled by the brand management team." Where has control shifted? To the boys in shipping?

Brands need "the freedom to breathe and change to survive." Hello! Hasn't product innovation and change been at the heart of all great branding from time immemorial!

And so I ask myself: Despite all the jargon, has technology and the internet really changed the rules of branding? Can a small company really expect to brand at warp speed? And what is there to learn from Intel's $500 million dollar branding campaign when your entire marketing budget is $500, $5,000 or $50,000?

"Instant" brand leadership is a fantasy, so don't even go there. You're not a rap artist. In the business world brand leaders are built over time. You can certainly speed up the process with an innovative product that causes a sensation in the marketplace with the help of an imaginative marketing campaign. Remember why I'm standing here lecturing to you!

Every so often a product is introduced that causes a sea change overnight, particularly in the world of technology. Think of Intel, Microsoft, Oracle, and Cisco. But this is the exception, not the rule. You budding entrepreneurs have to realize that the branding process is slow and seductive. Only hard working, patient types who understand how to control perception are the winners.

⊃⟩ ⊃⟩ ⊃⟩

Chapter Nine
Just what is branding anyway?

As I said earlier, **everyone today wants to be a brand leader, build brand equity, maintain brand loyalty, and avoid brand dilution.**

But just what does branding mean, anyway? Let's try to sweep away the myths and get down to some basics.

Branding began with consumer-goods – the things you buy in supermarkets. It was soaps, snacks, and Alka-Seltzer. Procter & Gamble, Colgate-Palmolive, General Mills, and Nabisco were five of the gods. Brand managers lived in places like Cincinnati, and Minneapolis.

But now, branding has spread to every industry. Companies that sell widgets want to differentiate themselves from the competition; to stand-out from the incredible number of choices overwhelming consumers; to be players in worldwide markets. Brand managers are leaving Cincinnati for Seattle to brand Boeing and the like.

Remember earlier, I mentioned that the world of branding is full of jargon? For all of you budding Brand Managers, I'd like to offer some simple, concise explanations.

A brand according to *Webster's Third New International Dictionary* is "a class of goods identified as being the product of a single firm or manufacturer...for instance, well known brands of canned foods." Campbell's Soup is the leading brand of soup, and Coca-Cola is the leading brand of soft drink.

Barrons Business Thesaurus defines brand in a visual manner as a "badge, brand name, crest, emblem, ensign, hallmark, identification, imprint, insignia, label, logo, logotype, mark, marker, motto, name, representation, seal, sigil, sign, signet, stamp, symbol, tag, trademark."

The One-Day Marketing Plan says that "a brand is composed of the title or name by which the product is commonly known, and graphic forms of identification, including symbols, logo types or signatures, tag lines, or characters."

In his book, *Marketing Management*, Philip Kotler, professor of marketing at the Kellogg School of Management at Northwestern University, says that "The art of marketing is the art of brand building. If you are not a brand, you are a commodity. Then price is everything and the low cost producer is the only winner."

Here's how The BullsEye Branding Method sees it:

Building a brand is the control of perception...to develop brand leadership, and brand loyalty, and *prevent brand erosion.*

The entire world of production and manufacturing of *any* product or service exists to control our needs and wants...to convince us that we, as consumers, need a particular product or service. To not just want x soup, but a particular brand of soup with a *known* name and a *familiar* label. We believe in it. We trust it. We buy it.

Brand leaders know, respect, and never lose sight of their customers. They know their needs, their wants, and their desires. Inside and out. McDonald's works hard to lessen lost revenues due to poor customer service, but is it working? Like I've said, if the employees don't understand how perception affects them in their personal lives, how can they understand, and appreciate, the impact that perception has on the golden arch?

Brand leaders know the power of perceived value.
A polo shirt sporting the logo of a popular brand costs three times (or more) than a polo shirt from a discount store costs – even though the two shirts are of comparable quality. Perceived value is a psychological commitment that has little to do with practicality.

Brand leaders know how fear impacts perception.
Any product having to do with children, food, health, safety, security, and our finances are particularly susceptible to perception fueled by fear. The food industry is extremely concerned about studies that are health related. Anything having to do with cancer or the heart. Oatmeal and orange juice are beneficiaries of positive perception. Genetically modified foods are being undermined by negative perception.

There are different types of brands:

A manufacturer's brand is one in which a company produces many different products all under one umbrella brand name. Heinz, Nike, Kraft, Betty Crocker, etc. You see this most often with consumer packaged goods and also high-tech software products such as Microsoft, Intel, and Oracle.

One company can also produce many different brands. General Mills makes Wheaties cereal and Bugles snacks. Procter & Gamble manufactures many different brands that compete with one another in the same product category – Tide and Cheer, for example, are both laundry detergents.

Private label branding occurs when the wholesaler or retailer puts their own name on a product or products made by one or more manufacturers. Private label brands are usually lower in price than their competition. You trust the store, so you trust any product with the store's name on it. Kenmore at Sears, for instance. One of America's most successful chain of supermarkets, Wegmans Food Markets, is renowned for their private label branding of everything from dog food to Italian food. It's generic gone upscale!

A brand can be international, national, regional or local in scope. You can find a McDonald's everywhere, from Poland to Beijing, but you have to go to Staten Island to find Nunzio's Pizza!

The benefits of branding to the consumer include trust and confidence in the product quality, consistency, and price. You know exactly what you are looking for. A brand may also evoke a sense of status. The logo on your shirt, on your golf ball, Tiffany on a gift box. It's amazing what we will pay for "perceived value."

The benefits of branding to the company include giving "added value" to a product, building brand equity and loyalty, standardizing advertising and packaging, eliminating confusion amongst different products in a line, and the consumer's willingness to pay a higher price. It still astonishes me how much my fans will pay for Wicked Wyoming Chicken Marinade!

Brand loyalty is just what it says. Edwin Wilkerson, the father of a dear friend of mine, would use only Gulden's Mustard. Absolutely no other mustard would do. I feel the same way about Hellmann's Mayonnaise.

Brand equity is a combination of brand awareness and brand loyalty built over time. It represents the sum total of assets and liabilities associated with a brand name – very hard to quantify, but easy to destroy if not carefully nurtured and protected.

Brand erosion is one of the negative consequences resulting from brand equity being challenged by competition and changes in the marketplace. Brand erosion is to be avoided at all costs! Great brands are not built overnight, but it is shocking how quickly a great brand can be undermined. K-Mart, for instance.

Brand association is anything linked in the consumer's or client's mind about your brand. Tiger Woods and Nike; Bill Cosby and Jello. It also results from awards and other forms of recognition such as when a company wins the prestigious Malcolm Baldridge Quality Award.

Now that you know the jargon – tell me, what do each and every one of these terms have in common? You got it – **they're all about the control of perception.**

Elements of a brand identity include:

The name – directly related to what your business is or does, and how you wish to be perceived. Remember the Christianity example I gave.

The symbol – a visual manifestation of the basic essence of a brand instantly understand-able and memorable. The Cross, for example.

The slogan – blessedly brief, to the point, and memorable. A summation of the three words that describe your brand in a positive manner. Father. Son. And Holy Ghost.

The positioning statement – one sentence that succinctly sums up the benefits of your product or service, and what differentiates it from the competition. Christianity didn't do this, but you should.

The mission statement – what you believe in; what you are committed to; your values as a corporate entity. The Apostles' Creed.

Brand *marketing* is a different subject dealing with sales strategies, advertising budgets, packaging, promotions, and the like. A marketing program – regardless of its size or scope – must be built, however, on the foundation of a brand identity that never loses control of perception.

You gain control of perception by practicing The BullsEye Branding Method, and learning the 7 Rules of Perception.

The power of perception to create and maintain a brand identity is the same whether you are a Fortune 500 such as Nike or a small start-up shoe company in Sandusky. A common error of the big boys is to think that they're somehow different. They aren't.

Chapter Ten
Three Major Branding Myths

1. Being "first to market" is vital.

Being first sounds like a good idea, but first *in* can oftentimes become first out! Priceline.com, for example. Priceline created the concept of naming your own price on the internet, but the hype of what they offered was not what shoppers experienced in reality. So Priceline's credibility shot down (along with their stock).

At the turn of the 20th century, the Rockefeller fortune was built on John D. scooping up "first to market" gas stations all over Ohio. Now at the beginning of the 21st century, the same is true. Established retailers are gobbling up the ideas created by upstart e-tailers.

The "old economy" boys (& girls) were bright enough not to rush into anything.

Wal-Mart faced daily criticism from "New Economy" gurus for not rushing into the internet with Wal-Mart.com. The retailing giant took their sweet, "Old Economy" time before dipping their toe into the brave new world of e-tailing.

Merrill Lynch did the same. They watched dot.com start-ups like etrade and Ameritrade, and when they saw proof that consumers liked the concept of making their own discount trades on the internet, Merrill sprung their own immediately successful website.

General Electric is last, but certainly not least. CEO, Jack Welch – admitting that he didn't comprehend the internet until 1998 – watched some of his best and brightest executives jump ship for the lure of instant riches with dot-com start-ups. But Jack got them back! G.E. quickly incorporated the internet into its basic business processes to create greater productivity and profits. As Jack said in *Newsweek*: "There's no such thing as Old Economy or a New Economy. We owe the dot-coms an enormous debt. But clearly, big companies like ours are the biggest beneficiaries."

Truer words were never said. It is no accident that the *Fortune* magazine list of the Top 10 brands includes G.E. and Wal-Mart. Not one single dot-com is on the list.

2. The bigger your marketing budget the better.

This concept is also meaningless if your credibility is low. Priceline.com again, for example. Even Captain Kirk as spokesperson and hundreds of millions in advertising couldn't keep this instant internet brand from imploding.

The same was true for other upstate dot-coms. All those millions of dollars spent on grossly oversized advertising campaigns could not save mortgage.com, garden.com, drugs.com, and toys.com.

3. The internet is revolutionizing the rules of branding.

While it is true that the internet has created some major branding successes in short periods of time such as Amazon, ebay, and Yahoo, the internet super highway is littered with scores of major branding failures. Faced with one dot-com, "new economy" debacle after another, a glut of competing web sites, and no evidence that side bars translate into sales, brand managers slashed their budgets and rediscovered the tried and true branding concepts that actually worked – and kept the sales pipeline pumping!

Even without MBA's and the benefit of branding consultants or the internet Levi-Strauss, Gail Borden, and Joseph Campbell instinctively knew that:

1. Perception *is* Reality.
2. Controlling perception on a consistent and persistent basis is *essential*
whether you are:
a word-of-mouth brand,
a street brand,
an internet brand,
a huge business,
a tiny start-up,
a politician,
a movie star
someone looking for a great date
or the perfect mate.

The same principles apply.

PART FOUR:
THE BULLSEYE
BRANDING METHOD ™

Chapter Eleven
The Power of Your Name

Now that you know what branding is, and what it isn't, it's time for me to return to the really juicy part of the story – namely how I became the Chicken Billionaire.

As I mentioned before, when I first started bottling Wicked Wyoming Chicken Marinade, I knew that I didn't have a clue about creating a brand identity. So I called my friend, the Eagle, who taught Brandin the Bull how to succeed using the 7 Rules of Perception.

First thing the Eagle said to me was: "Look here, Kyle Otey, I'm not here to play games. You've got a great product in Wicked Wyoming Chicken Marinade, you've got a catchy name – but that's about it. Without any money you're going to have a hard time bringing this product to market no less become a brand leader. But, as you know I can't resist a challenge, so I'm going to sign on as your consultant for no pay. I'll take it in stock when you go public."

"Well, what do we do now," I asked the Eagle? "You've got it right. I don't have a plumb nickel to market Wicked Wyoming Chicken Marinade."

"If we can't outspend 'em," the Eagle replied, "we'll just have to outsmart 'em! So let's put on our thinking caps and get to work developing an innovative brand identity program."

The Eagle reviewed the first three rules of perception:

Rule 1: Perception *is* Reality.
How any person perceives any brand
is his or her reality - whether fair or not.

Rule 2: Powerful Influences.
Many factors influence how anyone
or anything is perceived.

Rule 3: The Rule of Three.
How any brand is perceived tends to be reduced to three descriptive words that may be positive or negative.

"Now I'd like you to think about the power of your name. Many of the greatest brands were named after their founders. Levi Strauss and Levi jeans. William Colgate and Colgate toothpaste. Joseph Campbell and Campbell Soup. George Eastman and Eastman Kodak.

"Small towns all across America had storefronts proudly featuring the family name. Earl's Drugs, Wegmans Food Markets, Hamm's Meat Market, Darlene's Beauty Salon, Sansone Chevrolet. But my, how times have changed. Nowadays, personal names have gone by the wayside when it comes to branding," the Eagle said with some regret in his voice.

"How come?" I asked.

"It's simply not sexy. Brand consultants today like to make up names that I have a hard time pronouncing.There's the fear of litigation, and its spill-over effect on the family name. Imagine Elbers Telcom a synonym for scandal instead of Worldcom...Kowlowski Enterprises the object of law suits instead of Tyco.

"But I predict that Martha Stewart sheets will be on beds all over America ten years from now. I'm buying her stock. Most brand consultants don't agree with me, however. The thing to do is to create names that mean virtually nothing. "No matter how I try to make Phillip Morris, Altria...it just doesn't sink in. It's the A thing. Brand consultants seem to like names that begin with Al: Altria, Alleve, Allegra, Algeria. I can't keep track of it all. Which is a drug? Which is a tobacco? Which is a country?

"So let's go back to the time when the name of the founder was the name of the company.

Elizabeth Arden	Samuel Colt
Clarence Barron	Charles Crane
John Jacob Bausch and	John Deere
Henry Lomb	Jack Dempsey
Ephraim Bigelow	Abner Doubleday
Alpheus Bissell	Clarence Henry Dow
Gail Borden	George Eastman
David Dunbar Buick	George Washington
Joseph Campbell	Marshall Field
Robert Agustus	Harvey Firestone
Chesebrough	Henry Ford
Gaston Chevrolet	Alfred Carl Fuller
Walter Percy Chrysler	King Camp Gillette
James Boorman Colgate	Adam Gimbel
Peter Fenelong Collier	Charles Goodyear

Henry John Heinz
Charles Elmer Hires
Walter Hunt
James Johnson and
Robert Wood Johnson
Charles Herbert Kraft
Sebastian Spering Kresge
Edward Drummond Libbey
Frederick Louis Maytag
Cyrus Hall McCormick
Philip Morris
Ransom Eli Olds
Elisha Graves Otis
Frederick Pabst
James Ward Packard
Arthur H. Pitney and
Walter Bowes
Theron Tilden Pond
George Mortimer Pullman
Frank Perdue
Eliphalet Remington
Paul Revere

Richard Joshua Reynolds
Richard Warren Sears and
Alvah Curtis Roebuck
Helena Rubenstein
Horace Andrew Saks
Jacob Schick
Charles Scribner
Isaac Merritt Singer
Albert Goodwill Spalding
Levi Strauss
Henry and Clement Studebaker
A. Fabian Swanson
Gustavus Franklin Swift
James Walter Thompson
Charles Lewis Tiffany
Philo Remington and
John Thomas Underwood
George Westinghouse
Oliver Fisher Winchester
Frank Winfield Woolworth
William Wrigley, Jr.
Linus Yale

VS.

Tom Siebel of Siebel Systems, Michael Dell of Dell Computers, and Ken Keithley of Keithley Instruments.

Before we decide on a name for your new company, think what it would be like if it featured your name. You must believe in your business, product or service as if it is your own identity. Your slogan, your positioning statement, your vision, and mission must have as much meaning as if your own name was on the line. All the great corporate leaders believe this, even if their name isn't that of the company. Lee Iacocca and Chrysler, for instance. And my buddy, Jack Welch, and G.E.

Chapter Twelve
Evaluating the Strength of Your Own Personal Brand

The BullsEye Branding Method begins with the innovative idea that **in order to understand the power that perception plays in brand leadership, you must first understand how perception controls the success of your own Personal Brand identity.**

One of the absolute, core competencies of any brand leader is the brand awareness of its employees. Every single member of the organization – from the front office to the receptionist – must understand the impact that he or she has on their company's brand identity; and truly value the bottom-line impact that perception has.

"This knowledge must come from the bottom UP – not from the top down," the Eagle insisted. "Company after company makes the mistake of dictating the importance of brand awareness, and customer satisfaction. This comes off as a self-serving lecture about profit and loss.

"When this knowledge comes from the bottom UP, your bottom line improves. Every employee in your company will know that in each and every customer interaction, how he or she is perceived is vital to the success of the brand. That,
I AM the brand!

Rule 4:
Know Yourself

**Know the three words
that best sum up
your brand in a
positive manner.**

You learn your three words by doing the Personal Branding Exercise.

"This is true empowerment," the Eagle observed. "This is what self-realization is all about. You realize the power of perception in your interactions with others...and you understand how perception impacts your ability to succeed. **What's in it for me?**

"Once you appreciate the power of perception in your own personal life, you can better understand the power of perception in your new company's brand identity. In Maslow's Theory of Motivation (so influential in marketing to determine what motivates people) self-actualization is at the top of the pyramid of needs. Without self-actualization, training is useless.

The Personal Branding Exercise sensitizes individuals to the power of perception in determining attitudes about co-workers and customers alike. It works equally well with training that is based on achievement knowledge (learning about yourself) and specialized knowledge (becoming brand aware).

This is step one of The BullsEye Branding Method. Everyone must do the Personal Branding Exercise - even if you're the CEO!

Personal Branding Exercise #1

Please answer each of the following questions in 1 minute or less. It is important that you put down what first comes to mind.

1. Using just three words (or short phrases) describe how you perceive yourself:

_____   _____   _____

2. Using just three words (or short phrases) describe how you think you are perceived by others:

_____   _____   _____

3.Using just three words (or short phrases) describe how you would most like to be perceived by others:

_____   _____   _____

4. Using just three words (or short phrases) describe how you would most NOT like to be perceived by others:

_____   _____   _____

**5. If there is a difference between perception and reality (how you answered questions 1 through 4)
why does this gap exist ?**

_____   _____   _____

6. Name three things that you can do that would help close the gap between perception and reality?

_____   _____   _____

7. Name three things that could PREVENT you from closing the gap between perception and reality?

_____   _____   _____

The Personal Branding Assessment is on pg. 115.

Chapter Thirteen
Branding Someone You Know

After I finished the Personal Branding Exercise and studied my answers - some of which surprised me - the Eagle said, "Now use the same exercise to describe someone you know." Then have whoever you select do the same exercise with yourself as the subject."

"Wait just a minute," I blurted out. "What's this going to accomplish? Let's get on with the brand identity program."

"First things first," the Eagle replied. "Doing both exercises is what makes the BullsEye Branding Method so revolutionary. You cannot understand the power of perception in brand identity and brand awareness training until you fully understand how it works in your personal life. It's one thing to pick your three words. It's quite another to have another person see you the same way."

This is why the Personal Branding Exercise and the Branding Someone You Know Exercise have such impact in brand awareness, sales, customer service, leadership, and diversity training.

"By doing both exercises you learn the importance of Perception *Inside* and Perception *Outside* being united. Without internalizing this knowledge, there is little chance of a person truly appreciating the power of perception in product branding. There are no short-cuts if you want brand aware employees. You either get it, or you don't," the Eagle said quite matter-of-factly.

Not wanting to appear clueless, I agreed to do Exercise #2. Like a dummy, however, I picked Mama Otey to brand me. It felt like being a turkey trussed up for a Thansgiving feast! "So that's what you think of me, Mama?"

"Get a life, Kyle Otey," Mama declared. "Do you want this marinade to make us a million, or not? This is my ticket to paradise so don't blow it!"

The logic finally sunk in. Exercise #1 and Exercise #2 became the foundation of every bit of training that I do with my Wicked Wyoming staff.

I came to realize that it makes no sense to separate brand awareness, sales, customer service, team building, leadership, and diversity training.

They're ALL controlled by perception.

Exercise #2: Branding Someone you Know

*Please answer each of the following questions in 1 minute or less.
It is important that you put down what first comes to mind.*

1. Using just three words describe how you view (person you select):

_____   _____   _____

2. Using just three words describe how you think   _____
perceives his or herself.

_____   _____   _____

3. Using three words describe how you think _____
would like to be perceived by others:

_____   _____   _____

4. Using three words describe how _____would
most NOT like to be perceived by others:

_____   _____   _____

5. If there is a difference between perception and reality (how
you answered questions 1 to 4) why does the gap exist ?

_____   _____   _____

6. Name three things that _____ could do that
would help close the gap between perception and reality?

_____   _____   _____

7. Name three things that could prevent _____
from closing the gap between perception and reality?

_____   _____   _____

The Personal Branding Assessment is on pg. 116.

⟫ ⟫ ⟫

Chapter Fourteen
Creating A New Brand Identity

Now the real fun began – namely creating the brand identity for Wicked Wyoming Chicken Marinade. First we reviewed the first four of the 7 Rules of Perception:

Rule 1: Perception *is* Reality. How a person perceives any brand is his or her reality – whether fair or not.

Rule 2: Powerful Influences. Many factors influence how anyone or anything is perceived.

Rule 3: The Rule of Three. How anything or anyone is perceived tends to be reduced to three descriptive words that may be positive or negative.

Rule 4: Know Yourself. Know the three words that best sum up your brand in a positive manner.

"Next is the issue of **control**," the Eagle said. "Remember, you're the new kid on the block. No one yet knows who you are. But, once you introduce Wicked Wyoming Chicken Marinade, you've got to be ready to move quickly to control perception."

"This is why every single member of the Wicked Wyoming Chicken Marinade Staff must be brand aware from day one. And I mean everyone.

"Being in control of perception begins INSIDE your business. Lack of information creates a vacuum, and when there is a vacuum your perception will be created by others. Your competition, your customers – worse yet YOUR OWN EMPLOYEES – will fill the vacuum with misinformation that will, regrettably, become the reality by which you are perceived. Trust me, this is a huge mistake. Do not dilly-dally around, Take charge."

Rule 5:
Don't Lose Control

If you let others define your brand, their perceptions may be full of misinformation

which is very difficult to change.

The Eagle's advice about the importance of remaining in control of perception and not letting my competitors seize the playing field made a lot of sense to me. So did this next piece of advice:

"You know how we all have our favorite brands of cars, soaps, and soft drinks?" the Eagle observed. "We remain loyal to the brands we believe in, and that is why they are brand leaders. Trust is a huge part of building brand loyalty and brand equity.

"Trust is established when there is unity between how you perceive Wicked Wyoming Chicken Marinade and how others perceive it."

This is PvP
Perception *Inside* versus Perception *Outside*

"When there is unity between Perception *Inside* and Perception *Outside*, your brand has HIGH PvP. **When there is a disconnect between how you view your product, and how others view it, the result is conflict, confusion, and missed sales.** You are the victim of LOW PvP. No amount of money spent will be successful until this disparity is resolved.

"The great brands are very consistent and persistent in the way they are perceived – and their manufacturers make darn certain that it stays that way. Jello is Jello. And Kleenex is Kleenex. What you see is what you get. Both have HIGH PvP.

"Customers remain loyal to brands they know and trust."

Rule 6:
The PvP Principle

**There should be
unity between
Perception *Inside*
versus
Perception *Outside*:**

*how you perceive
your brand versus how
others perceive
your brand.*

At last I was ready to create the three words that would shape the identity of Wicked Wyoming Chicken Marinade.

Exercise #3: Creating A Brand Identity

1. Using just three words, describe Wicked Wyoming Chicken Marinade:

_____   _____   _____

2. Using the three words in question 1, describe Wicked Wyoming Chicken Marinade in one sentence. (If you can't describe your brand in less than ten seconds, you've lost your audience).

_____

_____

_____

3. Using three words, describe how you would most like Wicked Wyoming Chicken Marinade to be perceived:

by employees

_____   _____   _____

by customers

_____   _____   _____

by vendors

_____   _____   _____

by competitors

_____   _____   _____

4. Using three words, describe how you would most NOT like Wicked Wyoming Chicken Marinade to be perceived:

by employees

_____   _____   _____

by customers

_____   _____   _____

by vendors

_____   _____   _____

by competitors

_____   _____   _____

5. Name three things that you can do to insure that Wicked Wyoming Chicken Marinade has high PvP:

_____   _____   _____

6. Name three things that could PREVENT your being able to control how Wicked Wyoming Chicken Marinade is perceived?

_____   _____   _____

The Brand Identity Assessment is on pg. 117.

Once I'd created the three words that best express Wicked Wyoming Chicken Marinade in the most positive manner possible, the Eagle next made sure that I understood the importance of **consistency**.

"The three words that you chose to sum up the attributes of Wicked Wyoming Chicken Marinade will guide the development of your positioning statement, your slogan, and its application to every ad, promotion, and press release that you do from here on out. I cannot stress this enough. The average consumer is deluged daily with a massive amounts of information. You can't stand out from the competition unless you insist on maximum consistency in the way you express your brand identity.

Stick to message.

"It's the trust factor again. Remember that the reason that Al Gore lost the presidency was because he kept changing his three words every debate. We never did know who the real Gore is. Karl Rove and the rest of the Bush camp made sure that George stuck to message. If you think it was boring, guess what – Bush is president!

Rule 7
Be Consistent

The three words
that best describe your brand
should be expressed with
confidence and
consistency

PART FIVE:
MY FIRST BILLION

⯈⯈⯈

Chapter Fifteen
I Feel Wicked

Whenever I started to stray from following the BullsEye Branding Method, Mama Otey kept me on track. "Study the elements of a brand identity program and I'll treat you to Mama's Wicked Wyoming Turkey Tetrazzini tonight." That got me back to basics fast.

The positioning statement – I turned the three words that I'd created in Exercise #3 into one sentence that sums up the product's benefits and differentiates it from the competition. This is the 10-second sell: Wicked Wyoming Chicken Marindade is shamelessly and sinfully intense in flavor, originality, and quality.

The name – Wicked Wyoming Chicken Marinade: Wicked = it's so good, it feels wicked. Wyoming = free-spirited individualism.

The symbol – a visual manifestation of the product that is instantly understandable and memorable. My face! Move over Betty Crocker.

The slogan – "I Feel Wicked." Every time you see those three words you think of Wicked Wyoming Chicken Marinade. Whatever happened to the concept of putting the name of a product in the slogan? You Can Be Sure If It's Westinghouse. Diamonds Are Forever. See the USA in your Chevrolet. Put Some Hungry Jack In Your Life. These days, marketers spend millions and no one remembers what the ad is selling!

The mission statement – here, I was inspired by Carly Fiorina, CEO of Hewlett-Packard. She said, "If we took the mission statements of 100 large companies, mixed them up while everyone was asleep, and reassigned them at random, would anyone wake up tomorrow and cry, 'My gosh, where has our mission statement gone?'" Way to go, Carly!

So here we had all the basics down pat, but we still didn't have a dime to our names. I wasn't about to do one of those "the biggest reason for small business failure is undercapitalization" scenarios. As the Eagle so aptly put it: "If you can't outspend 'em, outsmart 'em."

We made t-shirts with the Wicked Wyoming Marinade logo on the front, and put our slogan "I Feel Wicked" on the back. Then we sent them to a bunch of Hollywood stars who are into animal rights. Susan Sarandon was the first big score. She was snapped wearing our t-shirt and the photo ended up in *People* magazine. Soon Harrison Ford, Sharon Stone, Barbra and the whole bunch of activists were wearing Wicked Wyoming t-shirts. Even J. Lo wore it when she was interviewed on *Entertainment Tonight* before her wedding.

Before we knew it Wicked Wyoming Chicken Marinade was showing up at every sit com and movie set and sales were booming.

Then one morning I got a call from the White House saying Bush wanted to fly me down to the ranch for a barbeque with Putin. Next day, there was this big color photo on the front page of the *New York Times* with the President holding a bottle of my marinade!

Bush started giving "I Feel Wicked Gift Kits" to heads of state whenever they visited the ranch. The Middle East sheiks went so nuts for it that Air Force One had a standing order for a case of my marinade. Opening day of baseball in Cuba, Castro was spotted wearing a Wicked Hat.

We'd gone international!

⤳ ⤳ ⤳

Chapter Sixteen
The BullsEye Branding Audit

After such a heady beginning you can imagine how tough it was to stay in charge. Our little business took off quicker than a wild turkey and growing pains soon set in. I was traveling night and day hawking the marinade from coast to coast. Hunters who used to shoot me on sight now wanted me to join their parties! Sold a lot of marinade by schmoozing with the food industry biggies at Jackson Hole shoot outs.

Meanwhile, back at headquarters, Mama Otey was having a tough time keeping everything under control. We had so many new employees that we couldn't train them properly and I suddenly got the sinking feeling that I was guilty of the Eagle's #1 sin: losing control of perception. Perception *Inside* was disconnecting from Perception *Outside*. It was time to bring back the Eagle.

Brand leaders do market research, consumer surveys, analysis of customer service records, reports from the field, and updates on what the press is saying (or not saying). And this is all well and good, but sometimes all of the info gets in the way of clear-headed analysis.

The BullsEye Branding Audit,

however, uses the Rule of Three to help companies of *any size* maintain brand equity, brand loyalty... and prevent brand erosion. It's easy to do, easy to measure, easy to compare, and it works worldwide. You can continuously evaluate the strength of your PvP and use the results to guide decisions on what needs to be updated, or changed to maintain control of perception. I credit the Audit with putting Wicked Wyoming Chicken Marindade on the road to brand leadership. And if I can do it, anyone can, Mama Otey says.

I use the Audit for Brand Awareness, Sales, Customer Service and Diversity training

I can hear you Fortune 500 biggies saying, "Well this is fine for small businesses who don't have sophisticated internal marketing systems and branding consultants." But you are precisely the ones who *most* need to understand that **Perception *is* Reality...The power of The Rule of Three....and the wisdom of PvP.**

Beware of the guru game

Some are suspicious of concepts that make sense to both CEO's *and* switchboard operators... who know that perception is based on human nature... and that the control of perception is what branding is all about. Please resist the urge to think that you are too big for something this simple and this understandable.

Chapter Seventeen
Repositioning

Wasn't long before Mama Otey had moved from Branding Audits to being a cult figure in the fast track world of cuisine. Diane and Charlie began cooking with her once a week on *Good Morning America*. She was a regular on David Letterman. Producers were fighting over her to do a show on the Food Network. *Gourmet* did a 10-page spread on "Wicked Ways with Poultry." *The Wisdom of Mama Otey Cookbook (Let's Talk Turkey)* hit the best seller list knocking off a Junior League cookbook from Charleston!

Wicked Wyoming Chicken Marinade was one of the most pervasive **one item** brands in food history. But tell me, how long can you do just chicken? Our BullsEye Branding Audits gave us early intelligence that our loyal customers were getting restless. Even my staff was complaining. The receptionist had the gall to write on her Audit that the three words that best described Wicked Wyoming Chicken Marinade were boring, boring, and more boring. Competitors left and right were closing in. It was time to reposition.

Be forewarned. While perception is fluid and changes over time, it is difficult to change in the short term. But since staying in control of perception means that you have to act fast if you see your brand eroding, once the handwriting is on the wall you can't be out chasing a golf ball. If you take on repositioning, do it with purpose and passion, or don't go there!

Once we see a brand as low priced, it is difficult to raise the price. And once we are used to the taste of a product, it is difficult to get used to a new flavor. Cola-Cola's attempt to change their formula with "The New Coke" was one of the greatest (and costliest) branding fiascoes in history.

The great brands are so resistant to change, in fact, that they think the most *minor* change in packaging is revolutionary (as when Campbell's updated their labels and General Mills updated Betty Crocker's hairdo). And right they are, for there is a delicate balance between maintaining the status quo and attempting to change a brand. Consumers claim that they like change, but they also like things to stay just the way they are.

Making any changes to an existing brand must be done with great care.

In September, 2003, Eastman Kodak shocked investors by slashing its generous dividend from $1.80 to 50¢ . Why? To finance a much needed repositioning from film to digital. Kodak stock plummeted 20% in two days. Repositioning is tricky, so be prepared!

Today's world is obsessed with change, and consumers are fickle – well at least the young ones are. The need to bring new products to market at warp speed, and the ability to tap new tools such as the internet to increase productivity (as well as to analyze the marketplace) are revolutionizing the speed with which new products are being introduced. Sometimes too quickly.

Why didn't Corning change its name?

Here you have a company whose name was virtually synonymous with cookware. The maker of some of the 20th century's greatest Super Brands such as Pyrex ware and Corning ware. In the mid 1990's, Corning had to make a critical decision about its future. Its coveted patents had expired and competitors worldwide were knocking off cheap versions of their products. Profit margins were decreasing in the consumer products division.

Little did the public know that Corning's famed Research Center had, for decades, been experimenting with glass ceramics (the very elements that made Corning ware possible) and a little known field called fiber optics. Their scientists were busy creating innovative products that had revolutionary potential in communications and other exploding markets.

Corning management made a bold and daring decision. They sold their *entire* consumer line including every *single one* of the products that made their company famous for more than century. And seemingly overnight, Corning morphed into a high tech company dedicated to fiber optics! Amazingly, Corning did not change their name to Fibersys or Optizoom. They changed *everything but* their name!

The rest is history. In one of the stock clubs that I am a member of, I recommended that we buy Corning stock in 1999 because of the potential of the new high tech company that Corning had evolved into.

We made a bundle as did many other happy investors.

Then in 2001 the stock market imploded and so did Corning stock. And did they change their name? No. I find this fascinating for they had every excuse in the world to do an Andersen Consulting and become Accenture, to be like AOL Time Warner and drop the AOL, or be MCI Worldcom and drop the Worldcom.

Was Corning right to stick with their name? I think so and so does Mama Otey. She's wedded to her Pyrex ware.

In the case of Wicked Wyoming Chicken Marinade however, there were legitimate reasons for changing our name. We followed the BullsEye Branding Method like it was a ritual. We did the Repositioning Audit with our staff, our customers, and our loyal consumers. We evaluated our positioning statement, name, symbol, slogan, and mission statement as though we were starting all over again.

It didn't take too long for us to make a decision. Drop the word chicken. The rest seemed to be working.

)))))))

Chapter Eighteen
Changing a Brand Gone Bad

The repositioning campaign was a wild success. Before long we had marinades of every variety and sauces for beef, seafood, pork, chicken, pasta and rice. We created regional varieties to suit every taste bud. We had hot and sweet, sweet and sour, mild and extra hot, you name it – we were product segmentation gone amok!

Kyle Otey Inc. went public and the Eagle became a millionaire overnight. Mama Otey retired to her villa in the south of France – right near Julia Child's place – but not before the FDA investigated her claim that our marinades had therapeutic benefits and should be used at least three times daily.

I got into buying art and played a lot of golf with my buddy, Jack Welch. At one of our outings in Nantucket I spotted a yacht that I liked. Tried to buy it and the owner wouldn't sell so I bought the yacht company. Before I knew it, Kyle Otey Inc. was buying up electronics companies, plumbing supplies, even a line of designer jeans.

My nephew was now in charge of the Branding Audits and it was he who warned me that Kyle Otey Inc. was suffering from brand dilution. The SEC was also sniffing around for a poster boy for reform. It was time to bring the Eagle out of retirement.

"You've strayed too far from your core competencies," was the message. When the Eagle speaks, I listen, and here's what I learned about why brands go bad:

Product defect
When reports surfaced about deaths caused by defective Firestone tires this was bad news indeed to the millions of people who trusted one of America's greatest brands. Even worse was the way Firestone lied about it.

Product tampering
Remember the Tylenol incident? A shocking case of product tampering that put a respected brand synonymous with trust into jeopardy. Tylenol had nothing to do with the tampering, but they had everything to do with the way they reacted.

Competitor introduces better product or service
When Michael Dell introduced a quicker new way for computers to be custom configured to the customer's exact needs, he revolutionized the computer industry overnight.

Technology becomes obsolete
PeopleSoft's best selling software products became obsolete, and the company found itself in the position of either reinventing itself or going out of business. It chose the former.

Couldn't deliver the goods as promised

Apple spent millions hyping its new, updated iMacs. Then customers waited and waited for the computers to show up in showrooms. Customers hate to have their expectations squashed.

Inept leadership

Xerox went into a slow and steady decline as it attempted to adjust to the digital age. But, as is so often the case with brands gone bad, disgraced leaders at Xerox were rewarded with multi-million dollar, lifetime "golden parachutes" as the company's stock plummeted and employee pensions were decimated.

Undercapitalization

The #1 reason for small business failure.

Poor customer service

It never fails to amaze me how many companies disregard how important consumer confidence is to brand equity and brand loyalty.

Being a brand leader is never having to say, "we're sorry."

In Japan to lose face was the ultimate disgrace. You took your own life rather than embarrass your family, your business, or your government. It was called committing hara-kari.

American CEO's are not quite so dramatic. They simply say "I'm sorry" and quit with a golden parachute. It's the thing to do when your brand has gone bad. Firestone apologized for its defective tires. Worldcom apologized for Bernie Ebbers. President Clinton apologized to the American people for his sexual dabblings.

But simply saying "I'm sorry" does not save a company or a person whose brand has gone bad. Without meaningful internal analysis and corrective action, no amount of money spent or empty words will suffice. Do not lecture about greed and corporate reform, and then do "a Grosso!"

If there is any problem with your product – move quickly to do damage control, to communicate with your customers openly and honestly, and to make changes that are meaningful and believable.

In sum:

Do what Tylenol did to their bottles. They implemented new tamper proof packaging and, in the process, retained their high brand loyalty.

Do what the egg industry did when medical reports started linking eggs with high cholesterol. They promoted the nutritional aspects of eggs while also creating low cholesterol and no cholesterol substitutes.

Do what I did.

Kyle Otey Inc. went back to its core competencies. We sold off all the companies that were unrelated to marinades and sauces. I sold my yachts, jets, and art collection and donated the money to the Sierra Club.

The truth set me free.
I moved quickly to create a positive   perception
of change both internally with my employees and
externally with my customers and shareholders.
When a brand identity is believable, it is inspirational.
Particularly in today's world.

The rest, as they say, is history. Mama Otey is back in
Wyoming volunteering her time to animal rights causes.

And me? I'm the Ambassador to Turkey.

PART SIX:
SUMMARY

)))))))

Personal Branding
Exercise #1 Assessment

a. Compare the three words you chose in Question #1 to the three words you chose in **Question #2** to determine your PvP, how close Perception *Inside* is to Perception *Outside*. How you view yourself in Question #1 should be *close* to your answers in Question #2. If your answers are close together, you have HIGH PvP, and a STRONG Personal Brand identity. If your answers are far apart, you have LOW PvP, and a WEAK Personal Brand identity.

b. Compare the words that you chose in **Questions #2 and #3**. Again, how you think others perceive you and how you would *like* to be perceived should be as close together as possible. Are your answers close or far apart? The closer they are the HIGHER your PvP, and the STRONGER your Personal Brand identity. The further apart your answers are, the LOWER your PvP, and the WEAKER your Personal Brand.

d. Question #5 is revealing. You are providing yourself with important information about what you need to do to change, and to bring Perception *Inside* closer to Perception *Outside*. The third word you chose is often quite telling – perhaps the most difficult word for you to admit to, and acknowledge.

e. Question #6 is the beginning of self-actualization – of being perceived as you truly are. These three words form the foundation of your action plan for change. They describe what you believe you can *realistically* do to bring Perception *Inside* closer to Perception *Outside*.

f. Question #7 is another aspect of self-actualization. It shows what you are afraid of – what you think may *prevent* you from becoming the person you want to be perceived as. These three words are hard to accept, but *must* be overcome if you want to change how you are perceived.

Branding Someone You Know
Exercise #2 Assessment

a. Compare the three words you chose in **Question #1** to the three words you chose in **Question #2** to determine how close Perception *Inside* is to Perception *Outside*. How you view the person you described in **Question #1** should be close to your answers in **Question #2**. If they are, the person you selected has HIGH PvP, and a STRONG Personal Brand identity. If your answers are far apart the person you selected has LOW PvP and a weak Personal Brand identity.

b. Compare the words that you chose in **Questions #2 and #3**. How you perceive the person you selected, and how you think he or she would like to be perceived, should be as close together as possible. Are your answers close or far apart? The closer they are the HIGHER the PvP, and the STRONGER the Personal Brand identity of the person you selected. The further apart your answers are, the LOWER the PvP, and the WEAKER the person's Personal Brand Identity.

d. Question #5 is revealing. You are describing what the person you selected needs to do to change, and to bring Perception *Inside* closer to Perception *Outside*. The third word you chose is often quite telling – perhaps the most difficult word to admit to.

e. Question #6 describes what you believe the person you selected can *realistically* do to bring Perception *Inside* closer to Perception *Outside* – to be seen as he or she truly is.

f. Question #7 is another aspect of self-actualization. It shows what you think the person you chose is afraid of – what you think may *prevent* he or she from becoming the person you think he or she would like to be perceived as. These three words *must* be overcome if meaningful change is to take place.

Creating A Brand Identity
Exercise #3 Assessment

a. Question #1 should be three words that realistically summarize your business in a positive manner. If it doesn't then you need to take a good look at the three words you chose.

b. Question #2 should be the words in **Question #1** turned into a simple sentence. If anyone asks you what your business, product or service is, this is your 10-second answer – your positioning statement that succinctly defines who you are and what differentiates you from the competition. This one sentence should naturally lead to a conversation because what you say is interesting, provokes follow-up questions, and further discussion. If your positioning statement does not do this, then change it to one that does.

c. Compare your answers to **Questions #1 and #3**. Note how your answers in **#3** may vary depending on whether you are dealing with your employees, customers, vendors, or competition. In a healthy business with HIGH PvP, there's similarity in the answers. Are your answers close or far apart?

d. Your answers to **Question #1** and **Question #4** should be as *far apart* as possible. If they're not, your brand's PvP is in trouble right from the start.

e. Question #5 is the beginning of self-actualization These three words form the foundation of your action plan to develop HIGH PvP.

f. Question #6 is another aspect of self-actualization. It shows what you think may *prevent* you from achieving your goal of attaining high PvP. These three words are hard to accept, but *must* be overcome if you want to control perception and have HIGH PvP.

The 7 Rules of Perception

1. Perception is Reality
How any person perceives a particular brand
is his or her reality (whether fair or not).

2. Powerful Influences
Many factors influence how people form
their perceptions about a brand.

3. The Rule of Three
How any brand is perceived by any person
tends to be reduced to three descriptive words
that may be positive or negative.

4. Know Yourself
You, and every other employee of your
business must know the three words that
best sum up your brand in a positive manner.

5. Don't Lose Control
If you let others define your brand, their perceptions may be full of misinformation which is very difficult to change.

6. The PvP Principle
There should be unity between Perception *Inside* versus Perception *Outside*: how you perceive your brand versus how customers perceive your brand.

7. Be Consistent
Every employee must be able to express the threewords that best describe your brand with confidence and consistency.

Services

Educate! Inspire! Motivate!
• Inspirational books • Consulting
• Training programs • Merchandising
• Speaking Engagements

Topics include:
Brand Leadership
   Creating a Brand
   Maintaining a Brand
   Saving a Brand
Personal Success - How the 7 Rules of Perception
   can change your life
Customer Service - To the customer,
   "I AM" the brand. Starring Kyle Otey,
   Chicken Billionaire.
Corporate Change - Why we resist it.
Office Politics - Wanda Pensky and the
   Weasel, and other horror stories
Leadership - What you see is what you get.
Diversity - Combatting profiling and stereotyping.
Team Bulding - Using the Personal Branding
   Exercise to build self-awareness
   and communication.

Targeted programs for:

Fortune 500 companies   **Retail stores**
Small Businesses   **Restaurants**
Institutions and   **Hotels/Motels**
Organizations   **Real Estate**
Health Care   **Politics**

Multiple Applications:

Sales and Marketing
Building A New Brand
Maintaining Brand Leadership
Repairing a Brand Gone Bad
Customer Service Training
Sales Training

Management
Leadership Development
Organizational Development
Team Building
Corporate Change
Increasing Productivity

Human Resources
Recruitment
Employee Retention
Diversity Training
Office Politics

Memorable Merchandising

Combine your logo with the PERCEPTION RULES! logo, characters and themes applied to:

T-shirts	Hats	Mugs
Totes	Post-It Notes	Calendars
Posters	Pens	Golf balls
Bookmarks	Mouse Pads	Screen Savers
Reminder Cards		

Also available:
Animated videos;
Audio CD's and tapes.

Flexibility and Value:
• Turn-key as well as full service options.
• All books available in hard and soft cover;
  and short books.

Universal Appeal:
Since perception is based on human nature
PERCEPTION RULES! has worldwide applications.
Our books feature animal characters and stories
that cross over cultrual and ethnic boundaries.

Licensing Opportunities

Ask about our lucrative domestic and global licensing
opportunities to represent the Bulls Eye Branding
metod including PERCEPTION RULES! books,
training and consulting programs, and merchandising.

The Publisher of the PERCEPTION RULES!
series of self-help business books is

Visit us online at www.perceptionrules.net

Ordering

The PERCEPTION RULES! business library includes:

PERCEPTION RULES!
Personal Success
The Story of Brandin, the Misunderstood Bull

PERCEPTION RULES!
Brand Leadership
The Wisdom of Kyle Otey, Chicken Billionaire

PERCEPTION RULES!
Fear of Change
The Transformation of Melvin

PERCEPTION RULES!
Office Politics
The Story of Wanda Pesky and The Weasel

PERCEPTION RULES!
Customer Satisfaction
You ARE the Brand!
More Wisdom from Kyle Otey, Chicken Billionaire.

Acknowledgments

When Kyle Otey entered my life I found a master of marketing who was in total sync with my ideas, and it was he who provided me with the inspiration to develop this book. I can't thank him enough! And thank you Mama Otey for your cooking when I was busy writing.

Thank you my dear children, Ned and Kate, and my loving friends for believing in me, and standing behind me through thick and thin.

Some people were especially helpful as wise eyes and helpful guides in the editing and design process: In particular: Cynthia and Richard Hoskin and Jill Stolt, three of the most talented, caring, and sharing friends who I have ever had the good fortune of knowing.

Many of America's leading brand names are mentioned in the text – so many so that we decided to dispense with the inclusion of endless trademark and copyright symbols for the sake of readability. We do, however, honor their rights and know that you do, too.

A final word of thanks to Brandin the Bull who introduced me to Kyl Otey, and the Eagle whose wisdom is at the heart of so much of the advice in these pages.

PERCEPTION RULES!

V Harris

September, 2003

NOTES